Our Dancing Days

PATIENCE STRONG

Frederick Muller Ltd
London

Our Dancing Days

When we were young, my love and I – our dancing days went dancing by. So quickly did they hurry past – that we imagined they would last – forevermore: but suddenly – the music stopped for you and me, whirling around that lighted hall. The last waltz was the last of all. And even now . . . that melody – has power to quicken memory – and stir life's ash into a blaze – remembering our dancing days.

Sudden Bereavement

It opens before you: the desolate track –
that leads into nothingness, empty and
black . . . Suddenly all your tomorrows
have gone. You can't see the signpost. But
you must go on. Life for the moment a
bleak blank may seem – a rubble or ruins, a
meaningless dream . . . But you must go on
– every step of the way . . . when travelling
home at the end of the day – the lamp of
your faith in the dark you will see –
confirming the hope that "the best is to
be".

First and Last

The first time I saw you I'll never forget –
that very first moment when you and I met
. . . I felt it was meant for I knew at a glance
– that this wonderful meeting was more
than mere chance.

I'll always remember the first time we
danced – together – forever – enraptured,
entranced . . . The first time we sat at a table
for two – the very first time that a dream
had come true.

The last time I came to your hospital bed –
for just a few minutes, the doctor had said
. . . The last time of all – but my heart was
aware – of a joy that was deeper than death
or despair – knowing you'd gone but a few
steps ahead – out on the road that we all
have to tread.

Wedding Wishes

Blessings on the bride and groom; health and happiness – and a future that fulfils the wish we now express – the hope that Time will bring throughout the years that are to be – good friends, good days, good luck, good fortune and prosperity.

But more than all my life bestow its best and greatest boon – a happy home where love will always keep their hearts in tune – bound together in a bond of trust and sympathy – may it be a marriage based on peace and harmony.

The Quiet Haven

If only we'd waited a little while longer –
We might have kept trouble at bay . . . If
love had been deeper and faith had been
stronger – we might have been happy
today . . . But somewhere we blundered
and took a wrong turning. It happens. We
made a mistake – Time taught its grim
lesson too late for the learning. The
sacrifice now we must make . . . But in this
quiet haven to which we've been driven –
our peace we'll recover when all is
forgiven.

New

Time is a generous giver. It comes with a gift that's unique: a year that is fresh and unsullied, the date and the day and the week – have never been lived. They'll be new days; and oh what a chance is here – to atone for our sins of omission and make it a wonderful year.

Undeserving we take this endowment.
God grant, too, new hope and new heart – a
new kind of spirit within us – a new kind of
living to start . . . Now is the moment for
bringing a new age of faith to its birth –
laying foundations for building the
kingdom of heaven on earth.

That Smile

A face overflowing with happiness like a
pool that is brimming bright – with
bubbles of sparkling radiance, alive with
an inward delight. Rarely one sees a face
like this in these days of unrest and ill will. I
found it amongst my old photographs.
That smile! . . . It is haunting me still.

It plucked at a chord of memory. I swear I
can hear again – that laughter like rippling
water, evoking the streams and the rain –
of our walks in the border country and in
my mind I see – my young friend treading
the stepping-stones where the Ceiriog
meets the Dee.

One Day's Journey

Go your way with one day's load – but not
along tomorrow's road. You are not asked
to walk that track – until it's on the
almanac. Until today has faded out – you
do not need to think about – what
tomorrow's going to bring. A good
thought, that, to which to cling.

Do not face until you must – tomorrow's
problems – Let the dust – of one day's
troubles settle first. Don't anticipate the
worst. When the going's rough and tough
– One day's journey is enough.

One Little Cloud

A single cloud can thicken overhead – until
across the whole sky it is spread – North,
south and east and west it stretches wide –
the gold and blue of heaven's dome to hide.
One little cloud of doubt on life can throw
– a shadow that will deepen and will grow
– No joy can pierce the gloomy canopy –
that veils the sun whose face we cannot see
. . . O, think the best and let no doubts steal
in – to spoil the happy world that is within.
Let there be light. Let Love's own sun
break through – to open up a clearer, fairer
view.

Opportunity Lost

There's always a gap between the stones
where you can plant a seed – there's always
a chance to say a word or do the kindly
deed – that helps to lighten someone's load
along a rough stretch of the road.

There's always an opportunity your part in
life to play – but if you are self-absorbed
you look the other way – and leave it to
some other man – to be the good
samaritan.

All too often you pass by upon the other
side – uncaring or too busy, eyes averted,
on you stride – hoping someone else will
do – the thing that was required of you.

The Place
where I was Happy

They say you should never return,
pursuing the shadows of dreams. They say
you should never go back – however
inviting it seems – But places to me mean
so much – a house or a street or a view –
reviving the magical touch – of happiness
shared there with you.

They say it is folly to trace the steps of a joy
that has gone. They say, but for me it's not
true – for me the delight lingers on – and
where I was happy I know – that happiness
there will remain – And so to those places I
go – to live it all over again.

Winter Fantasy

Winter silences are deep. The earth with
frost is bound. Ice becalms the singing
brooks, and on the frozen ground –
snowflakes fall like fairy foam that piles up
feather-light – till every bush is hidden
under mounds of dazzling white. Winter is
the silent season, quietening the mind. You
who walk the country lanes a new delight
will find – as you tramp soft-footed into
scenes of fantasy – the well known way
dissolves into a world of mystery. The
blinding snow obliterates the
once-familiar view – and you are lost, a
stranger in a place you thought you knew.

First and Second Thoughts

You thought at first you knew just what to
do. No more shilly-shallying for you. You
thought you had decided for the best –
now that worry could be laid to rest – but
second thoughts came nagging in the night
– as you woke and wondered – was it
right? And as you quietly pondered it anew
– things seemed to change. You took a
different view.

Suddenly you saw the way ahead – an
unseen hand had cut the knotted thread –
of the web in which you had been caught –
And you were free! Thanks to that second
thought.

This Day is for You

There's light at the window. Another
night gone. A new morning breaks, so get
up and get on – with all that is waiting for
someone to do. Accept what it offers. This
day is for you.

So take it and make it and do what you can
– to gather some good from your brief
human span... So short is time's measure,
so big is the need – to seek and to find an
acceptable creed – to live out in all that you
think, do and say, your faith to declare in a
practical way... Not wasting a moment
mere dreams to pursue. There's light at the
window – This day is for you.

Coming Home to You

The thought that I am coming home to
you – runs through my mind in everything
I do. On the treadmill of routine I turn –
my daily living at the job to earn – and
when the going's hard, the outlook black –
I cling to this one thing: I'm going back –
back to the little home we've saved to buy
– One in a row – but well content am I – and
happy when I see that lighted door. Could
anybody ever wish for more? The weary
journey home, week in week out – makes
me wonder what life's all about – But
when I reach our number in the road – my
heart begins to sing. It's my abode –
Forgotten then the worries and the stress.
This is our place: our nest of happiness.

Was it Worth it?

Was it worth all the worry and fuss? Was it
worth all that trouble for us? Was it worth
all the tension and strain? Could we live it
all over again – should we make a quite
different move? What were we trying to
prove? Let's come down to earth and begin
by letting a new spirit in. Time's precious –
so why can't we try – to let the old
grievances die? –It's not worth the
heartaches and tears – wasting the best of
the years. Let's take what life offers and
live – and really forget and forgive.